DREAM JOBS IN SPORTS RETAIL

ALISON DOWNS

Rosen
YA
New York

Published in 2018 by The Rosen Publishing Group, Inc.
29 East 21st Street, New York, NY 10010

Copyright © 2018 by The Rosen Publishing Group, Inc.

First Edition

Library of Congress Cataloging-in-Publication Data

Names: Downs, Alison, author.
Title: Dream jobs in sports retail / Alison Downs.
Description: New York : Rosen Publishing, 2018. | Series: Great
careers in the sports industry | Includes bibliographical refer-
ences and index. | Audience: Grades 7–12.
Identifiers: LCCN 2017020610 | ISBN 9781538381465 (library
bound) | ISBN 9781508178651 (paperback)
Subjects: LCSH: Sports—Vocational guidance—Juvenile literature. |
Sporting goods industry—Vocational guidance—Juvenile literature.
Classification: LCC GV734.3 .D68 2018 | DDC 796.023—dc23
LC record available at https://lccn.loc.gov/2017020610

Manufactured in China

CONTENTS

Introduction — 4

CHAPTER 1 **Overview and Job Opportunities** — 7

CHAPTER 2 **Getting Prepared** — 21

CHAPTER 3 **Training, Internships, and Other Opportunities** — 36

CHAPTER 4 **Sports Memorabilia Retail** — 56

CHAPTER 5 **Sporting Goods Retail** — 67

CHAPTER 6 **Season Passes and Ticket Sales** — 80

CHAPTER 7 **Sports Advertising** — 90

CHAPTER 8 **Gym Front Desk** — 97

College and University Programs in Sports Retail — 104

A Career in Sports Retail at a Glance — 106

Bureau of Labor Statistics Information — 111

Glossary — 113

For More Information — 115

For Further Reading — 118

Bibliography — 121

Index — 124

INTRODUCTION

Sports fans are some of the most passionate people around! This crowd of fans cheers on the players at a Steelers game.

Whether you're playing on the field or watching from the bleachers (or even from the comfort of your own couch), there's no doubt about it—your life revolves around sports. Nearly every item in your closet has your favorite team's logo on it, you've turned down more invitations than you can count with the excuse, "Sorry, I have practice," and as far as you're concerned, Super Bowl Sunday should be a national holiday. So, naturally, when you consider all these points, it makes perfect sense that you are considering a job within the sports industry.

A job in the sports retail industry can be a dream come true for someone who wants to turn his or her passion into a career. The great thing about sports retail jobs is that many of them require minimal training, and that training is often available on the job, making this a great career for someone still in school or just dipping their toes into the job market. So don't sweat it if you've never had a job before—landing your first job in sports retail will allow you to get your foot in the door in a great industry.

Sports is a billion-dollar industry, and it's no wonder—everywhere you turn, you can see evidence of its far-reaching appeal; it seems nearly everyone owns something emblazoned with the logo or mascot of his or her favorite team. For a lot of people, watching sports is not just about entertainment—games are an important social event, bringing friends and family closer together … unless, of course, you happen to be rooting for the other team. Sometimes sports interest runs in the family, and children are encouraged to take part in the same sports their parents played.

Or maybe your experience with sports has been a little different. Maybe you've always been stuck watching from the sidelines and felt a little bit left out; maybe your grades in school weren't high enough to take part in team sports, or a medical condition kept you benched. Whatever the case, jobs in the sports retail industry can be a good fit for you, too, and give you an opportunity to rub elbows with others who love the world of sports as much as you do—you don't need to be a football hero to succeed at any of these jobs. And although there are many different jobs within the sporting industry, retail jobs are considered some of the most accessible. Retail jobs allow you to get your foot in the door and work your way up according to your own strengths. And like on sports teams, when you're part of a retail crew, you're part of a team—and as they say, a team is only as good as its weakest member. Retail, like sports, is all about teamwork.

Whatever your story, you have options. In the following sections, you will learn about several different career paths in the sports retail industry, as well as some easy ways to challenge yourself and gain valuable experience.

Chapter 1

OVERVIEW AND JOB OPPORTUNITIES

You eat, sleep, and breathe sports. You plan your days around sporting events (whether you're playing, cheering from the sidelines, or even watching from your couch), and the only thing that can spoil your weekend is a rain delay. If this sounds like you, you're already a perfect candidate for a career in sports retail. But what does "sports retail" really mean?

You may think that the sports retail industry is limited to a bunch of shoe and clothing stores at the mall, but it actually goes beyond that. Sports retail can be divided into a few different categories.

First, you have your standard retail job, which is exactly what you might find at your local mall or department store. These jobs include working for larger sporting goods chain stores like Champs Sports, Dick's Sporting Goods, Bass Pro Shops, Cabela's, Eastern Mountain Sports, Modell's, REI, and many others.

As a retail worker, you could deal with memorabilia, sporting goods, and more! Here, a sales associate adjusts a display of hats on the sales floor.

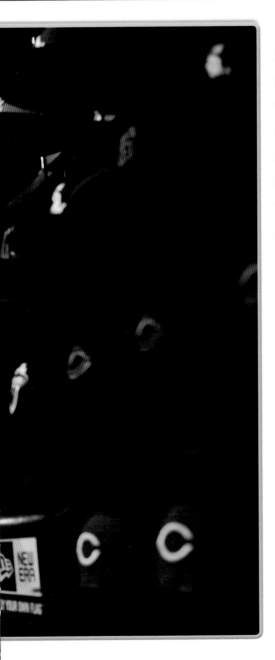

Then there are stores that are a little more specialized. You might work in a memorabilia store—these tend to be independently owned, not chain stores—or you might work in a store that primarily sells athletic shoes, like Foot Locker (and its smaller stores, Kids Foot Locker and Lady Foot Locker). There are even stores like New Balance that sell sneakers in a wide range of sizes and widths, as well as those to counteract foot pain, issues with posture, and more—these aren't your grandma's orthopedic shoes. Some towns might have smaller, independently owned sporting goods stores,

LANDING A
JOB INTERVIEW

Before you can even think about wowing the hiring manager, you'll need to figure out how to secure a job interview ... and it's not always easy. Here are a few tips.

- **Find the job you want to apply for.** You might see a Now Hiring sign on the door of the sporting goods store you frequent... but usually, it's not that simple—you'll have to do some searching. Websites like Indeed.com, CareerBuilder, and SnagAJob.com are good places to begin looking, but you can also check with your school—they might have a job board they can direct you to.

- **Update your résumé.** Once you find a job that looks promising, read the description thoroughly. Now take a look at your résumé. Does it clearly reflect your skills? Will someone reading it know you are right for this job? In the digital age, sometimes human eyes don't even see your résumé until later stages—larger companies sometimes employ programs that scan résumés for keywords, and your résumé might be discarded if it doesn't contain them. Take a look at your résumé again and see if you can insert any of the keywords from the job description. For example, if your résumé says you "ran a cash register," but the job you're

applying for wants you to have "customer service experience," swap out your
terminology for theirs—it basically means the
same thing, and it will get you past the hiring bot.

- **Write a cover letter.** Not everyone takes the
time to write a cover letter, so this is one thing that
will help you stand out from the pack. Again, using
keywords from the job description, write a little bit
about your experience and why you think you'd be
a good fit for this job. Sell yourself a little.

which cater primarily to school sports—fielding large orders for uniforms, shoes, and so on.

In addition to these, you also have sports retail jobs that involve sales, like radio advertising or selling tickets to events.

The greatest thing about most of the jobs in the next few sections? While they're all sports related, and having some preexisting sports knowledge will always come in handy, you don't have to be a sports whiz in order to do well at these jobs. If you have an interest in or passion for sports but haven't played much (or at all) and don't know Tom Brady from Tom Gordon, don't worry too much. Once you secure a job interview, just make sure your passion for sports comes through. You

can always learn any-
thing else you need to
know, and your passion
will help you stay inter-
ested and motivated.

WHAT EXACTLY IS THE DIFFERENCE BETWEEN RETAIL, SALES, AND MARKETING, ANYWAY?

The words "retail," "sales,"
and "marketing" are
sometimes used inter-
changeably in conversa-
tion, but they each have
some key differences.

Retail can be con-
sidered more of an "um-
brella" term—it could
mean someone who
works a cash register,
offers customer service,
stocks shelves, takes
inventory, and fulfills online orders. Someone who

Working for any retail store can help you get your foot in the door in the world of sports retail! Draw from your retail experiences during your interview.

works in retail may also be responsible for reaching certain small sales goals—but while this is considered part of his or her job, that person may not technically work "in sales."

Sales jobs are usually positions that are more focused on how many sales you are making. Sales goals tend to be larger, and you may even be paid on commission, meaning that you receive compensation when you make a sale. Salespeople are less concerned with how a store looks and more concerned with getting some face time in with customers: asking questions, assessing their needs, and selling them on a product. For example, a salesperson may be responsible for selling a certain number of pairs of sneakers per day, week, month, or quarter—or they may be responsible for upselling customers by suggesting add-ons or higher-ticket items. Salespeople might be responsible for cold-calling customers or bringing in their own leads. Some salespeople get paid an hourly rate, plus commission on any extra sales they bring in; other salespeople work on commission alone—which means that if they don't make any sales, they don't make any money. As you might imagine, salespeople who work on commission alone might be a little more aggressive when it comes to making a sale, and they might suggest warranties, credit cards, or even specific items.

Adam Hagerman, author of the blog *Walking to Wealth*, shared some of his experiences on his website. "When I was working on commission, I used to get a detailed report every payday. That report showed all of my sales and the exact commission that I earned on each item. Therefore, I knew what paid the best. So if you came into my store... I would focus my sales tactic on the product that paid me more money."

If you're friendly, like people, like to hustle, and don't shy away from a challenge, you'd probably be a good fit in a sales environment.

Marketing is similar to sales, but marketing jobs are usually performed a bit more behind the scenes. Working in sports marketing, for example, might require you to write ad copy, radio spots, or even plan and orchestrate Facebook campaigns. If you are a strong writer with an engaging voice, you'd do well to look into a marketing job. And if you're particularly great at persuasive writing but perhaps you clam up a bit at the thought of speaking to a customer face to face, you might want to consider marketing over sales. Social media marketing is a particularly hot career option that continues to grow along with social media platforms, with many companies paying good money to secure a social media specialist to run their ad campaigns, increase their overall reach, and update their pages daily.

MAKING A NAME FOR YOURSELF AS A SOCIAL MEDIA SPECIALIST

Go to Facebook and check out some of the businesses in your community. Do they have a strong social media presence? Can you identify ways they can improve? It's not surprising to sometimes find Facebook accounts that have been set up but largely ignored for years—sometimes businesses that are not social media savvy don't recognize the value of social media marketing. If you think you can help, don't hesitate to reach out to the company and ask if they're looking for a social media specialist or intern. If you're at all hesitant about your skills, there are lots of free online courses that will help you refresh your memory—check out Udemy.com and YouTube.

• Name Your Price

When approaching a business and offering to help, they'll usually give you an opportunity to name your own rate, which can be confusing if you've never worked as a social media specialist. Consider the work you'll be doing for them. For example, you should ask for more money if you'll be maintaining a website and a Facebook account—web design is a very specialized skill. Don't be afraid to ask for what you're worth—or even more than *you're worth. They may try to bargain you down to a rate they find more reasonable, so it doesn't hurt to aim high.*

- **Ask for Feedback**
When your relationship with a client ends, don't be shy when it comes to asking for reviews and recommendations. If you have a LinkedIn profile or website, that's a good place to post client reviews, or you can ask for typed letters of recommendation. If they were satisfied by your work, they may even recommend you to others—and word of mouth is the best form of advertising.

If you're already active across social media platforms like Facebook and Twitter, there are plenty of online courses (and even free YouTube videos) that can teach you how to extend your skills a bit further and effectively market yourself to companies.

THE TECHNICAL WORLD
OF SPORTS RETAIL

If you're as into computers are you are sports, you'll be excited to know that there might just be a position for you behind the scenes, too. As you may have noticed, malls, shopping centers, and even bigger chain department stores

The world of retail shopping is changing rapidly. Many consumers are choosing to make purchases online, causing numerous large chain stores to close their doors.

like Macy's and JCPenney are closing left and right, and many people are blaming these closings on the popularity of online shopping. Whether or not this is a trend that will be continuing remains to be seen, but if you're concerned, there are definitely a few things you can do to "future-proof" your career in sports retail. Much of the sports retail industry today is run online, so if you're computer savvy, you're in luck.

Many major chains, and even some smaller stores, have websites that allow customers to browse and purchase products online. These e-commerce sites need someone to set them up, someone to maintain them, and someone to pack and ship orders—other than that, software does the work of the retail store and employees and handles inventory management, as well, so you'll always have an idea of what's in stock and what isn't.

If you're interested in the web development side of things, you'll want to be sure you're taking IT and computer classes in school. Focus on web design, graphic design, PHP, HTML/CSS, and JavaScript. Learn about user experience design so you can best understand how to build an intuitive website, and pay attention to other e-commerce sites out there—what works well and what doesn't? Remember these factors so you can implement these designs if you plan on building your own site.

It might be that you're a people person and don't want to miss out on the customer service aspect of sports retail. If that's the case, you could even work during your free time, chatting or answering phone calls for sporting goods companies—without ever leaving your home.

"We still aren't at the point where all customers are comfortable using email or chat support, so phone support is still needed," says Tom Tostanski, customer experience associate at Nucleus. "For more complicated cases, you'll want to have the customer on the phone. If [a company] can't staff a customer service team in-house, it's easy enough now to hire people to answer calls from home."

If you wanted to be a doctor, the path you would take toward becoming one would be pretty straightforward, right? You'd take lots of science courses in high school, followed by more science and premed courses in college, then, finally, medical school, a residency, then a job as a full-fledged, board-certified doctor. But for someone who wants to work in sports, the path might seem a little muddier. Short of applying for a sports scholarship, adults might not always know the best way to advise you.

If you're still in school, it can sometimes be difficult to know exactly what to do next in order to pursue your dream. You might feel spread a little thin between classes and exams, and it can be overwhelming—especially if your peers seem to know exactly what they want to do. How can you successfully lay the groundwork for your future career? What are the next steps you should be taking? As it turns out, there are actually lots of things you can do to make con-

Career counseling is just one of many resources that may be available to you through your school. Don't hesitate to reach out to your counselors!

nections and gain some expertise while still in school. While you should be careful not to commit to too much and wear yourself out, don't limit yourself, either. Don't be afraid to try things that catch your eye—you never know what you might end up enjoying. "By the time I had finished my four years at ASU [Arizona State University], I had called at least 150 baseball games. I was the sports editor for the school newspaper and wrote a column called "The Hot Spot." Year-round, I also announced football, basketball, and some track meets as well," writes former sportscaster Al Michaels in his book *You*

Can't Make This Up: Miracles, Memories, and the Perfect Marriage of Sports and Television.

GET INVOLVED

Believe it or not, your community is probably the most valuable resource you have and a great place to start honing your skills and trying out new things. You might have luck coaching a little league team, running video cameras during football games, or even selling concessions at sporting events. Ask your gym teacher, a coach, or your guidance counselor if they can put you in touch with someone who might be able to point you in the right direction.

YOUR SCHOOL

Your school also comes equipped with a wealth of resources, so definitely check out opportunities available to you at your school first. Sometimes, it's easier to get your foot in the door when people already know you and can vouch for your character. If you're athletic, you can join one (or more) of your school's sports teams, or you could try starting your own after-school club if you can't find one that suits your fancy. If you prefer to watch games rather than taking part, you could offer to cover sporting events for your school paper, act as an equipment manager for a team, or even help coach.

Here, a basketball player and coach review a recent play. Being any kind of coach requires strong strategy, teamwork, and communication skills!

PARKS AND RECREATION

Your local parks and recreation website can be a great resource for sports jobs—paid or otherwise. Parks and recreation departments should be your first stop if you're looking for internships, coaching opportunities, volunteer hours, and more. You can sign up to be a scorekeeper, a tennis instructor… you name it, the odds are good that your local parks and rec are looking for someone just like you.

CABLE ACCESS TELEVISION

Most towns have a cable access—sometimes also known as community access—television station, which is run primarily by local

Playing softball for your town—or teaching it at your local parks and rec department—is a great way to make some like-minded friends.

volunteers. Often, the television crew will bring their equipment to community sporting events and record the action—sometimes even beaming it back live to the studio. Pay your local television station a visit, and see if you can be of assistance. They might need someone behind the camera, running the switcher, or maybe even someone in front of the camera to narrate the action or interview players. (This, particularly, might be a great way for you to make a name for yourself in your community.) Often, you'll need to take a basic training or video production course to prove you can safely handle the equipment, but after that, it's easy to get involved. The courses

Volunteering for your local cable access television station is a great way to learn new skills, and it can also give you an opportunity to rub elbows with some minor or local sports stars.

are usually free or low cost, so don't let finances deter you from checking them out. Pop in and introduce yourself, and make sure you explain your interests—they might have a special agreement with local schools in the area, and you might even snag some internship credits out of the deal.

Cable access channels are frequently looking for new programming, too, so who knows? What begins as a gig recording an early morning football game might turn into you hosting a weekly call-in show about sports.

With so many great options, you might be finding it difficult to decide exactly how to move forward. Don't sweat it. If you aren't certain where your talents might fit best, you could reach out to your guidance or career counselor, or maybe even your gym teacher or a coach. They should be able to talk you through things and help you figure out where your strengths lie.

INTERNSHIPS

Many high schools encourage juniors and seniors to take internships to get some practical, real-world experience— sometimes they even build internship time right into the school day, making it easy to take part even if you have an after-school job.

Check with your guidance counselor to see if you qualify for an internship, and then ask around.

INTERVIEW WITH CHRISTIE SULLIVAN, SOFTBALL COACH

How would you describe your relationship to sports?

I grew up playing mainly soccer, basketball, and softball. Sports was a big outlet for me, especially since I had untreated ADHD—I needed that energy outlet. It gave me structure and discipline and taught me teamwork and cooperation. I went to a Catholic school and [through sports], I got to meet kids from the public school, so I had a lot more friends than I would have [otherwise].

Now, my relationship to sports is [similar to] how I relate to life. I take a lot of the metaphors related to sports and apply them to daily life. For example, I was just talking to a student who is supposed to be graduating, but her grades are terrible right now. She plays softball, so obviously I'm going to appeal to her athletic mindset. I said to her, "If this were a softball game and we were down, would we just give up, or come up with a plan to make a comeback?" She agreed with the latter, and that made the situation seem more manageable to her. My therapist uses sports metaphors all the time to break concepts down for me so they seem more approachable.

What made you decide to become a softball coach?

I love playing [softball], and I love to relay that love to younger players who are learning the game and teach them what coaches ahead of me have taught me. You're not just teaching them about the game of softball, you're teaching them about life. It's a great chance to be an influence on a young adult's life in a positive way. I love being able to shape young people's lives in multifaceted ways. Seeing the impact I can make on them is very rewarding.

Your counselor may have one in mind, but you should also utilize your coaches, teachers, and other adults in your community. You could job shadow someone to see if his or her career is something that interests you. Internships are important at a college level, too, so it's great to start them in high school—it gives you some experience and allows you to have some practice under your belt, and it also looks great on a résumé, showing hiring managers (and college admissions departments) that you are mature and responsible.

DRESSING FOR YOUR INTERNSHIP

The way you present yourself is very important, even at an internship. You never know when you might run into someone important or if your internship might turn into a full-fledged job, so you should always take it seriously and make an effort to look your best. A nice pair of slacks, dress shoes, and a button-up or polo shirt or a dress or nice skirt is a good place to start. Depending on what your new responsibilities are, you may want to wear something that allows you a full range of motion. For example, a suit jacket wouldn't be a very comfortable choice if you're spending your evening stocking shelves.

• *Other rules may apply*

Besides the basic rules of grooming, some internships can be more strict about your appearance—especially if you're interacting directly with customers—so be sure to take into consideration how you're accessorizing. If you have facial piercings, you may be asked to remove them or wear a clear ring or stud instead. Some places even have regulations on things like nail polish color, hair length, and facial hair.

• *When in doubt*

When in doubt, it makes sense to overdress for your first day; once you have a better idea of exactly what you'll be doing (and what others wear on the job), you can alter your wardrobe and accessories accordingly. And if you're coming directly from school and won't have time to run home and change, you can always stash a clean shirt, some deodorant, and maybe even a toothbrush and toothpaste in your locker.

HIGH SCHOOL AND COLLEGE COURSES

You might not think your standard high school courses have much to offer you, but you're wrong. Pay special attention in your health classes, any classes that involve life science, and even statistics class—some introductory statistics classes are even using sports-related examples to help make things easier to understand.

Some colleges have partnerships with high schools that allow promising students to take college courses while they are still in high school. If your grades are fairly steady, you'd most likely be a good candidate for a program like this. Take a look at nearby colleges and see if they offer any courses that catch your eye, then approach your guidance counselor and ask if you'd be able to take part. They'll be impressed by your initiative.

Even if you find that you can't take college courses right now, that's okay. This is a great time to pay attention to your grades and put as much effort as you can into bringing them up as much as possible. If you plan on applying for college and want to take advantage of any scholarships, it's important to have good grades and good SAT scores—they will open doors to further opportunities. It's a good idea to work on polishing your writing skills, too. If you aren't a strong writer, you may want to enlist the help of a tutor or a writing skills center—ask your school if they can direct you to one. The right tutor will help you write, fine-tune, and edit your college admission essays, and even any essays that might be required for scholarship applications. If you don't have access to a writing skills center, speak to your regular English or writing teacher about other writing guidance programs or options.

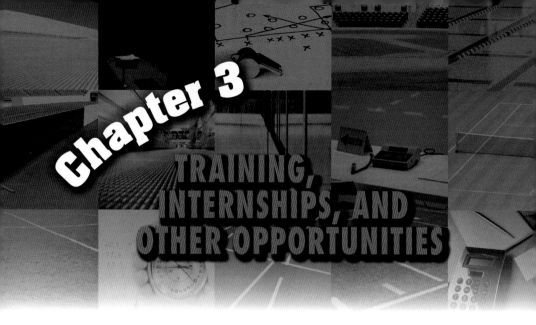

Chapter 3

TRAINING, INTERNSHIPS, AND OTHER OPPORTUNITIES

If you're looking to expand your knowledge of sports and really give yourself a leg up against the competition, there are a number of great colleges, courses, and internships that are worth looking into. While you may not necessarily need a college degree for most of the positions that are to follow, having some extra education never hurts.

COLLEGES

When it comes to sports, the college on everyone's lips these days is usually the University of Florida. Not only does the University of Florida lead the SEC (Southeastern Conference) and score a top-ten ranking in Academic All-Americans, they also have one of the best student fan sections in the NCAA (National Collegiate Athletic Association). This college has many notable alumni, including Tim Tebow, Cam Newton, Emmitt Smith, and Ryan Lochte—just to name a few.

The University of Florida offers degrees in sports and fitness, as well as related degrees in food science and human nutrition; physiology and kinesiology; and tourism, recreation, and sports management. And if you decide you've found your calling in retail and sales, they even have a marketing degree.

Southern states boast a large number of colleges with strong athletic departments, but if you'd rather be up north, you still have some options. The University of Connecticut scores decent rankings and is a standout in Division 1 sports. At UConn, you can major in athletic training, exercise science, or sport management. UConn graduates who are well known in the world of sports include Rebecca Lobo, Diana Taurasi, Ray Allen, and Khalid El-Amin, among others.

Moving northwest, Michigan is another great place to consider: they have the University of Michigan and Michigan State University, both scoring high for athletics. University of Michigan notable alumni include Tom Brady, Michael Phelps, Derek Jeter, Chris Webber, and coach Jim Harbaugh.

If movie stars and palm trees are more your style, look no further than the West Coast. The University of California, Los Angeles (UCLA) might be just what you need. Though at present time, they don't offer any sports-related undergraduate majors, they

Carolina Panthers quarterback Cam Newton speaks at a 2016 press conference. Normally comfortable in front of cameras, Newton received criticism for giving short, clipped answers following a Super Bowl loss.

still have something to boast about. UCLA has the proud distinction of having earned more NCAA titles than any other university. Some alumni include well-known names like Jackie Robinson, Troy Aikman, Kareem Abdul-Jabbar, Arthur Ashe, Michelle Kwan, and Jackie Joyner-Kersee, among others.

If you're interested in "going pro," and sports retail is just a fallback, you might want to try for a sports scholarship. Keep in mind, full sports scholarships are incredibly rare, but you might still get a partial scholarship—or even a merit award. To become eligible for a

APPLYING FOR A SPORTS SCHOLARSHIP

Practically every inspirational sports movie out there involves some talk of athletic scholarships—but how do you actually go about applying for one? They aren't just handed out like candy to every star quarterback. So while you shouldn't count on getting a scholarship, here are some tips on how to get started if you want to at least be in the running.

Register with the NCAA and NAIA Eligibility Centers. This is easy to do online. Just set up an account at each site, enter your school info (including ACT/SAT scores and transcripts), and request your certification. Familiarize yourself with the rules and regulations—what classes do you need to take in order to remain eligible? What do your test scores have to be? What about your grade point average (GPA)?

- **Create a video that showcases your skills.** Similar to a highlight reel that actors make when auditioning, your skills tape should show your best plays and showcase your skills and the variety of athletics you play. Post your video online, and include the link in your résumé and in your NCAA and NAIA profiles.

- **Research the schools you want to apply to and reach out to their coaches.** Email the coaches expressing interest in their schools, *and include your résumé and skills tape. If you don't hear back within a week or two, follow up. Once you connect with a coach, ask thoughtful questions about the school and its athletic programs to show you've done your homework, and be sure to be professional at all times.*

- **Read up.** *The NCAA and NAIA both have PDF handbooks called The Guide for the College-Bound Student Athlete. Take a close look at both of them (they're different, even though they have the same title), and familiarize yourself with their content—it might come in handy.*

sports scholarship, you'll need to register with the NCAA and NAIA Eligibility Centers in order to be approved—then you'll need to do some research to make sure the classes you take keep you academically eligible.

While you're still in school, there are many opportunities you can look into—check to see if your school (or community) needs someone to videotape sporting events, or perhaps even write sports articles for a local paper. All experience is important, so even if you aren't getting direct experience in a retail setting, these are great résumé builders that will both help you learn valuable terminology and make you stand out during an interview. And who knows? You might find your next hobby this way.

ALTERNATIVE COLLEGE MAJORS AND COURSES OF STUDY

If you choose a college that's known for its athletic department, you don't necessarily need to major in sports and fitness—in fact, some colleges with strong athletic departments don't even offer sports-related majors. There are a number of other majors that you might be interested in looking into, including:

- **Nutrition**—You can't expect a body to keep in optimum condition if it isn't being fed the

Proper nutritional information is not always common knowledge. Studying nutrition will give you the skills you need to help your clients live healthier lives.

proper nutrients. Majoring in nutrition will give you the opportunity to help yourself and counsel other athletes to help them eat the optimum diet for his or her body type, activity level, and overall goals. "The foods and beverages athletes eat can beef them up or lean them out, energize them or slow them down, keep them going or cause them to waiver midway through a workout, or even keep them playing instead of being benched due to illness," Jill Castle writes in her book *Eat Like a Champion: Performance Nutrition for Your Young Athlete*. "When thoughtfully planned, the foods we feed our athletes, and how we feed them, can fuel them to the next level of success."

- **Psychology**—Interested in what makes people tick? While it might not seem sports related, many of the jobs we've touched on—such as sales and marketing—rely heavily on understanding the human brain and identifying why people make the decisions they do.

- **Neurology**—There are many neurological studies being done regarding traumatic brain injuries that result from sporting accidents, so if the brain is something that also interests you, your thesis could always be on sports neurology or something similar.

- **Physiology**—Physiology is the study of body parts and their intended functions. A degree in physiology could set you up for a career in sports medicine or even massage or chiropractic care.

- **Retail Management**—If you love the idea of working in (or owning) your own store— whether it be a sporting goods store, collectibles shop, or something else—a degree in retail management is a great way to truly learn the ins and outs of the retail marketplace. You don't necessarily need a degree in retail management in order to work your way up the retail ladder—on-the-job experience is hugely important, too—but a degree couldn't hurt.

- **Marketing**—Marketing is part social media, part sales, and part psychology. Identify the needs of customers, figure out what makes them tick, and then write effective, successful ad copy. A degree in marketing would make you an asset in the sports world and beyond, although it will be particularly useful if you prefer to work behind the scenes… either in the marketing department of a large business, or being a marketing team of one for a small community shop. A marketing degree would also come in handy if you plan on going into business for yourself—you'll learn how to make a brand, cultivate a following, and how to start things off on the right foot.

WORK-STUDY POSSIBILITIES

When you start college, you'll be given an option to sign up for work-study opportunities, which are usually simple tasks, like manning a security desk or working in the cafeteria. These jobs are generally done in exchange for a

Getting work experience while you're a student can sometimes be tricky, but work-study is a great opportunity to build your résumé.

small amount of money or a small tuition deduction.

When applying for work-study opportunities, be sure to keep a lookout for positions that might give you experience in sales—like a school bookstore or gift shop—or sports, like keeping score, carrying equipment, or perhaps even making phone calls for your college team. You might be stuck doing something undesirable—like laundry for the football team—before you're able to work your way up to something better. Stick with it if you can; it not only builds character, but others will see you maintaining a good attitude and (hopefully) be impressed.

Are these students playing polo without horses? No, they're actually playing quidditch, a game created by author J. K. Rowling and made popular in the Harry Potter series.

COLLEGE SPORTS

Once you're in college, there are a wealth of options for getting involved in sports. Be it on a Division I team, at the student paper, or just tossing a football around with your roommates, college campuses have it all.

Schools of all sizes may participate in various NCAA sports. Usually, it's necessary to be recruited out of high school to make one of these teams, but if space is available, players may walk on—or be chosen in an open tryout. Many famous professional athletes started out as walk-ons, such as Scottie Pippin, Ozzie Smith, and Santana Moss. Keep in mind, though, that the NCAA has strict academic requirements, and playing on a university team is demanding. Make sure you're up to the challenge if you want to try out.

School teams also require a lot of support staff. Some of these roles go to students studying sports management or medicine, but others may be open to volunteers. Ask your school's athletic director if you're interested in pursuing this.

CLUB AND INTRAMURAL SPORTS

Some schools have club teams. These teams aren't sanctioned by the NCAA and are usually open to anyone who wishes to play. These teams play against other schools in friendly competition.

TOP TWENTY ATHLETIC COLLEGES

Choosing a college is a very tough decision to make—and it's a really important one, too. While there are tons of colleges that have great athletic departments, they aren't all created equal—so you should take your time and research your options thoroughly before choosing which schools you want to apply to.

Location
Consider what sort of area you want to live in (urban, rural, or suburban), what type of weather you enjoy (sure, living in Florida is awesome if you love the warm sun and being close to beaches—but could you handle missing out on snow and the changing of leaves?), and whether the overall feel of the school appeals to you.

Friends and Family
Do you have friends or relatives at any of the schools you are considering? Since you might be nervous about being on your own for the first time, you could always look into a college where you'll know someone, or at least shoot for one where you have friends or family close by. On the other hand, you might be excited to get away and start fresh in a school where no one knows you. Nothing wrong with that, either.

If you're feeling overwhelmed and need some help figuring out where to start looking, here is a list of the top twenty highest-ranking athletic colleges in the United States.

1. University of Florida
2. University of Alabama
3. Louisiana State University
4. Florida State University
5. University of Texas at Austin
6. Ohio State University
7. University of Oklahoma
8. University of Maryland, College Park
9. Auburn University
10. University of North Carolina at Chapel Hill
11. Michigan State University
12. University of Southern California
13. University of Miami
14. Duke University
15. Texas A&M University
16. University of Kentucky
17. University of Louisville
18. University of Connecticut
19. University of Tennessee
20. Baylor University

If none of these particular options catches your eye, that's okay—there are still a ton of other schools left to choose from. Do some research, narrow down your options, and start planning some college visits to see if you like the campus.

Often, you'll find clubs on your campus for sports that don't have an official university team or for sports that aren't recognized by the NCAA, like unicycle football and kickball. Some schools even have quidditch teams.

You'll also find intramural sports on campus. Anyone who signs up gets to play, and multiple teams are formed to play against each other. Students come up with clever team names, recruit friends to cheer,

Photography is a great way to get involved with sports, even if you aren't particularly athletic. Good photographers should be somewhat flexible, though, so do your stretches!

and play many different sports against classmates. Keep an eye out for sign-ups.

STUDENT MEDIA

If playing sports isn't your thing, but you like to write or talk about campus sports, you can always look into student media. Most schools have a student paper, and some

Spectating is a great way to support your favorite teams while also taking a peek at some of the roles people play at sporting events.

even have radio or television stations. If you're considering working in these fields after graduation, there's no better place to start getting experience.

While you probably can't expect to be a featured columnist or have your own radio talk show right away, many contributions will be accepted. Cover some sports that aren't getting a lot of ink in the paper, or see if you can help out with any live broadcasts of games. Start small.

SPECTATING

Finally, simply supporting sports on your campus is a great way to immerse yourself in them. Go to a game, and find a sport or two to follow—many schools offer discounted or free tickets for students to attend games, and club and intramural sports are usually free to watch. Show up, and cheer your friends and classmates on.

Chapter 4
SPORTS MEMORABILIA RETAIL

I f you love chatting with fellow loyal sports fans, working in a memorabilia shop will feel less like work and
more like fun. After all, you'll be getting paid to help outfit

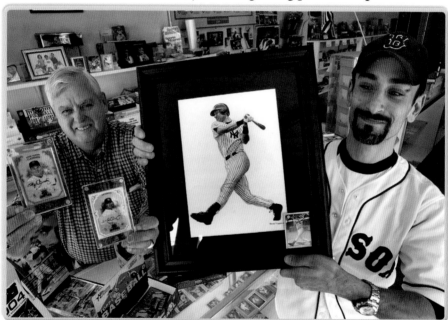

A memorabilia shop clerk and a Red Sox fan proudly display some of their baseball
mementos, including an original painting of Derek Jeter that was eventually used on a
baseball card.

fans in the jerseys of their favorite hockey players or for hunting down a photo from a very specific game and having it framed.

YOUR ATTITUDE DETERMINES YOUR ALTITUDE

Pete Rose may have been banned from professional baseball in 1989 after accusations arose that he bet on baseball games—including his own team. But, despite this, Rose is still able to rake in the dough as far as collectibles are concerned. And even though the market is fairly saturated with memorabilia signed by Rose (which means that there isn't much money to be made by reselling these items), he still manages to make a good living, selling each autographed item for sixty dollars, more than most other retired players who aren't in the Hall of Fame. So what exactly is the draw?

"What people keep buying is not just the autograph, but the experience of getting it," writes Kostya Kennedy, author of Pete Rose: An American Dilemma. When it comes to witty banter, Rose is unmatched; whether he's doling out advice to young athletes, telling stories, or poking fun at himself, it's Rose's attitude and personality that keeps fans lining up for a quick chat and an autograph.

There's also the scandal to take into account—betting on baseball games, especially on your own team's games, is a big deal—Rose is something of a polarizing figure, both famous and infamous, depending on whom you ask. "Rose...has the lure of an outlaw hero," writes Kennedy. No matter what you think of him, it's safe to say that Rose has continued to make a name for himself with his snarky stories and ability to laugh at himself.

There are a few different types of memorabilia stores—there might be one at your local mall—usually smaller chains or independently operated stores. But there are also much larger memorabilia stores at sporting arenas.

WORKING IN A MEMORABILIA SHOP

The day-to-day duties of a memorabilia shop employee will depend on a couple of factors—namely, time of year and the location of the shop. Memorabilia shops located in malls, casinos, and shopping centers tend to see most of their sales take place during the holiday season. This makes a lot of sense—after all,

Shown here are the corporate offices and year-round gallery of TheStadiumGallery .com, located in Sarasota, Florida. The Stadium Gallery specializes in panoramic sports photography.

that's when all stores see a big jump in sales—and what do you get the person who has everything but really loves the Yankees? It's pretty easy to pick that Yankees fan up a Yankees hat or a signed poster and know that he or she will love it.

There are also memorabilia shops located in major sporting arenas—those stores tend to see more sales year round and do the most business immediately before a game, during breaks, and immediately following a game.

These two types of memorabilia shops are similar, but a little different, when it comes to sales and experience.

BEWARE OF FRAUD

If you work your way up in the ranks—or decide to open your own shop—you may find yourself in charge of purchasing memorabilia; if this happens, you'll need to keep your eyes peeled for things that don't look quite right. As it turns out, a large percentage of memorabilia is not actually authentic, and it can sometimes be hard to tell the difference. Sportsmemorabilia.com suggests, "One of the best things you can do to protect yourself from a scam is to get familiar with the signing habits of specific athletes that you'd like to include in your collection. Many athletes enter contract agreements

INTERVIEW WITH BRANDON STEINER, SPORTS MARKETER AND OWNER OF STEINER SPORTS

How did your background help launch Steiner Sports?

The entrepreneur part of [my background] was the key; at the time, [sports] wasn't much of a business, and I was always looking for things new and different to do when it came to work.

What do you wish you knew before starting your own business?

How to finance the business better, that borrowing money is a key part of business and not a negative, [and that] the importance of talent that you hire to work for you and the quality of your clients are key.

What's it like to be a sales associate at one of your locations?

I want them to think about what's going on in the world of sports that week that might cause an emotional connection with fans; how to get our clients something they might want based on that connection is very important to us. What products do we need to acquire that will match up to what's going on in sports that week or month?

What is the most rewarding part of your job?
[Getting] fans and customers closer to the game and creating lifelong memories for them by allowing them to meet [his or her] favorite player, and/or getting them something to remember that moment by... [that] is absolutely priceless.

What advice do you have for someone who wants to work in a memorabilia shop?
In order to become a great salesperson, you need to be a great writer, be Internet savvy, [and] understand IT, just to name a few. [You also need to know] the history of sports... [that's] key to understanding why things get collected. It's good to know Derek Jeter and Michael Jordan, but knowing about Oscar Robertson, Bill Russell, etc., is [also] essential.

with memorabilia retailers, where they commit to autographing product that will only be sold through that particular company. If an athlete falls under contract with a specific retailer, there's only one reputable source to purchase that player's memorabilia." If a transaction seems fishy, or too good to be true, it probably is—it helps to err on the side of caution.

You never know how far a photo you take will go! Lou Gehrig liked this photo on the right so much that he ordered tons of copies and signed them for fans.

DIFFERENT TYPES OF MEMORABILIA

The bulk of sales at memorabilia stores comes from clothing sales: T-shirts, hoodies, and hats emblazoned with a favorite team logo or jerseys—either personalized or a replica of the jersey of a favorite player.

If you take a look around, it seems that memorabilia shops tend to be smaller, locally run affairs, rather than chains or corporations. Sometimes people even run their own memorabilia shops from

If you're looking to work in memorabilia but aren't sure if you'll like it, selling some items on eBay is a good way to dip your toes in the water.

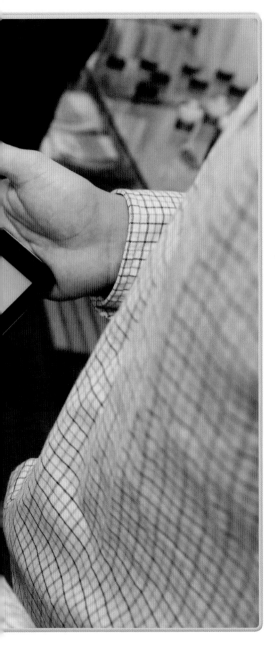

home, utilizing eBay, Amazon, and similar online services. So if it's your dream to own your own shop one day, don't be afraid to stop in on a slow day and have a chat with the owners. They might not offer you a job, but you'll gain valuable tidbits from picking their brains.

"No matter what business you're in, it takes many years to establish a business, build a reputation for yourself, and achieve success. It usually takes four to five years just to learn your industry and truly master the necessary skills. Then you spend another five to ten utilizing those skills, learning from the experiences you have, and growing your business," says Brandon Steiner in his book, *You Gotta Have Balls: How a Kid from Brooklyn Started From Scratch, Bought Yankee Stadium, and Created a Sports Empire.* If you're looking to be your own boss and start up your own shop, be prepared to work hard with little reward at first—success comes later, so be patient. Sometimes a business requires time to get off the ground.

Chapter 5
SPORTING GOODS RETAIL

With lots of different departments, working at a sporting goods store might be a good fit for you if you have lots of favorite sports or if you just prefer to shake things up now and again. You could run the outdoors section on Monday, selling camping and fishing gear, and then take your place in one of the more specialized sections the next day, helping some nervous parents outfit their new soccer player with shin guards and cleats. Alternatively, if you've played hockey your entire life, you might choose to stay in that department, answering questions that others on your team might not be able to field as thoroughly.

There are also smaller, more niche sporting goods stores—stores that focus primarily on footwear, like Finish Line, Champs Sports, Foot Locker, and Foot Action.

Sporting goods retail stores can have a varied selection. Some may center around team sports only, while others may branch out to include camping, boating, hiking, and more.

Athletes are nothing without their shoes, and athletic shoes make up 30 percent of all overall shoe sales in the United States. With so many kinds available, consumers might need a little bit of help to get the best fit and best style available based on their needs. That's where retail workers come in.

A DAY IN THE LIFE

In a lot of ways, working for a sporting goods store is similar to working for any other big-box retail store, like Walmart or Target. Though the exact terminology may be different from corporation to corporation, employees are divided into sales floor team members, back

INTERVIEW WITH MICHAEL PARISI, FORMER ASSOCIATE AT DICK'S SPORTING GOODS

How did you get your start at Dick's Sporting Goods?

I started at Dick's Sporting Goods my sophomore year of college [at] UMass Dartmouth. It was right down the street from my campus and was a job that provided flexible hours. What appealed to them about my schedule was my ability to work nights.

What's your relationship to sports?

I ran track in high school and college. I also played baseball, [both] in high school and for an amateur league in college. Dick's Sporting Goods was very interested that I was a student-athlete. They assigned me to footwear, as I could use my experience and relate to customers. I also worked in team sports and focused on the baseball section, as I was a former high school player and was an amateur league player during my tenure at Dick's Sporting Goods. My main focus was track and running.

What was it like to work at Dick's Sporting Goods?

I would punch in and then clean up from the previous shift. During my shift, I would assist customers. This consisted of either measuring their feet, grabbing shoes from the back inventory, or ordering items online for customers. It was also important to clean the *floor during my shift. If it was a slow night, we would be assigned projects or rearrange inventory.*

What advice would you give to someone looking to work for a sporting goods store like Dick's Sporting Goods?
I would tell them to have an enthusiasm for customer service. It may feel like you have long shifts and are not paid well, but you will learn how to interact with all kinds of people and will build a solid work ethic. Retail jobs are very team oriented, and you have a lot of support from coworkers and management.

room team members, front-end team members (this usually means cashiers), and managerial staff.

Front-end team members are typically responsible for welcoming customers, processing transactions (this could be sales if you work at the check-out lane or returns and exchanges if you work at a service desk), restocking the front lanes, and generally keeping the front of the store neat and tidy. By the time customers make their way to you, they have already made their decisions and are ready to check out, so you won't usually need to worry about being super knowledgeable

Retail workers do a lot more than run a cash register! Here, a salesperson helps a customer consider the pros and cons of two helmets before making a purchase.

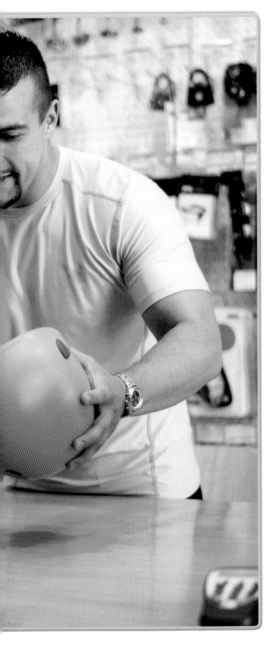

when it comes to the products. As a cashier, you'll usually be expected to be on your feet for the length of your shift (usually a minimum of four hours and a maximum of eight hours), and you should have the ability to lift around 50 pounds (23 kilograms). Scan and bag the customer's items while making some friendly small talk, and you're golden. Some stores might require you to ask customers to sign up for credit cards or rewards cards, but other than that, you generally won't be expected to memorize any sales pitches.

Back room team members tend to stay off the sales floor, mostly

IF YOU'RE LOOKING FOR PERKS, CHECK OUT E-COMMERCE RETAIL

Pro Athlete, an e-commerce company head-quartered in Kansas City, Missouri, has made a name for itself by selling bats and gloves for both baseball and softball. But that's not its only claim to fame—it's also considered one of the greatest places to work in retail. Pro Athlete not only treats its employees well (as is evident from the reviews on Glassdoor), it also provides them with a slew of fun benefits—including chef-prepared meals, a fitness center, a pool, a batting cage, and more. They also offer great health insurance, laundry services, and even free tickets to Royals games. As if all this weren't enough, the perk for celebrating your five-year anniversary with the company? Tickets to Walt Disney World.

With all these benefits, going to work sounds like more fun than staying at home, doesn't it? And although it might sound like the company is ponying up a lot of cash for these perks, the truth of the matter is that happier employees are actually more productive employees, who then work harder, are more loyal, and bring in more business. It pays to invest in your people. More and more businesses are realizing that employee happiness is vital, and they're making strides to ensure that work-life balance is made a priority. Even if they aren't able to offer

*killer perks like Pro Athlete, lots of busi-
nesses are now beginning to embrace some
smaller concepts, like the idea of unlimited vacation time. Employees can take as much vacation time
as they want in a calendar year, as long as they don't
abuse the privilege. Keep an eye out for things like
summer Fridays, too—where you can take a half or
full Friday off in exchange for working slightly longer
days during the week.*

counting and organizing inventory, unloading ship-
ments, building displays, and processing orders, all in
the warehouse. Back room team members might work
early morning or overnight shifts (especially during inventory time) or they may work when the store is open.
While some stores have a strict dress code and personal appearance policy for front-end team members—no
visible tattoos or piercings, no funky hair colors—keep
in mind that they may be a bit more lenient with these
guidelines when it comes to back room team members
who don't necessarily interact with customers.

Sales floor team members are very much the
outward face of any retail company, as these peo-

Sales floor team members may use electronics—like a tablet—to verify inventory. On busy days, they may even ring up transactions using them!

ple spend most of their time on the sales floor assisting customers. Their job can be as broad and varied as the needs of the customers, or they might be assigned a specific department. As a sales floor team member, you'll need to be friendly, enthusiastic, and really know your stuff. Customers will be coming to you with their questions and concerns, and looking to you to give them recommendations. Whether it's the highest-rated brand of soccer cleats or the newest mountain bike someone is looking for, you should be ready to offer your opinion on a wide range of products. "One of the most difficult things about retail is needing a passing knowledge about everything you sell. You can get most of the information you need from reading the box, but sometimes you need to know a little more. I don't play golf, but I need to be able to explain the difference between a soft glow ball and a harder one, and how they might affect your game," says Thomas Petrowski, zone manager at Walmart.

In a retail environment, managers usually start out as regular team members and work their way up, so the odds are you aren't ready to be a part of the managerial team just yet. But just for reference, managers usually supervise other staff, mediate customer disputes, delegate tasks, train employees, and follow up to make sure things get done. While lower-level associates might make sure the items are in the correct places, managers make sure that price changes are completed and products are being ordered to replenish things that are being sold. Managers are also able to make decisions in regards to price overrides and discounts on damaged items. Higher-level managers may even deal with hiring, employee performance evaluations, scheduling, safety concerns, and other things that make up the operations side of the business.

In short, lower-level associates are the face of the company, while mid-level managers make sure that products are being pushed to the sales floor and lower-level associates are assigned tasks. Higher-level managers focus on special projects, merchandising, and the behind-the-scenes work involved in running the store.

Chapter 6

SEASON PASSES AND TICKET SALES

Working for a ticket sales company, you would be the first place fans stop when they want to see their favorite team. Although the majority of ticket sales take place online these days, if you live in a major city, you've probably seen ticket booths or ticket resale shops near the stadium.

TICKET RESALE AGENCIES

Resale shops are the middle man, working as a third party to sell unused tickets, usually at a slightly marked-up rate. These shops make most of their money from season ticket holders who know in advance they won't be able to attend every game or show.

Ace Ticket and StubHub are just two resale agencies, but a quick Google search for your favorite team will turn up even more. These agencies are great to use when you want to pay a little extra to see a show or game that's been sold out for a while.

Sports are hugely popular all around the world. Here, Russian deputy prime minister Vitaly Mutko purchases tickets to the 2017 FIFA Confederations Cup.

GROUP TICKET SALES

Another way to get involved in the ticket market is to work directly for an association—for example, the National Basketball Association (NBA) might hire an account executive whose job it is to sell primarily to large groups. This is considered a more advanced sales job, so if you're interested in this, you should be very comfortable aggressively selling to people. Knowledge of sports is also important, and you're expected to have

If you're friendly and like to talk on the phone, you'd do well in a phone-based sales environment like at StubHub or Ace Ticket.

strong knowledge about the specific team you are selling for, so it helps if you're a quick study.

STRATEGIC SALES

If you can't see yourself on the front lines and dealing with customers, but you do have a strong understanding of sales, you might be a good candidate for the strategic side of the job. In a position like director of ticketing, you would be responsible for forming a strategic sales plan; forming, training, and coaching a staff; and

HOW TO LAND A JOB IN TICKET SALES

Find some companies that interest you. *If you live in a city, it might help to walk around near your stadiums—places like Ace Ticket have physical locations not far from Fenway Park, for example. You could always stop in for a quick peek and to gauge the atmosphere. If it isn't busy, feel free to have a chat with the employees there; their overall attitude can tell you a lot about their job satisfaction, and they might even be able to give you pointers on the best way to apply.*

Be sure to have an updated résumé and a strong cover letter when you're looking for jobs online—you'll need them!

- **Apply online.** Go directly to the company website and look for a jobs or careers section. If that fails, navigate back to the popular job search engines: CareerBuilder.com, Glassdoor.com, Indeed.com, and search that way.

- **Do your research.** Once you land an interview, make sure you are familiar with the company. What teams do they represent? Is their presence online only, or is there a brick-and-mortar location as well?

- **Be interview ready.** Dress professionally for your interview, be on time (early, even), and be ready to answer standard interview questions about yourself, as well as some sports-related questions. Ask thoughtful questions that show you have done your research about the company and are paying attention—try to be confident, but not cocky. You may also be asked to perform a computer proficiency test to show how well you can use some basic programs, like Word and Excel.

Follow up, but don't be pushy. If the interviewer gave you his or her business card, or if you've communicated with the interviewer by email, feel free to send a follow-up "thank you for taking the time to meet with me" email. If nothing else, it's a nice gesture that makes you stand out from the competition a bit.

making sure milestones are met. This is an even more advanced job, usually requiring two to five years of experience in the ticketing industry, so keep this in mind as a future goal you can work up to.

COMPANIES TO WATCH

If you're serious about sinking your teeth into the world of ticket sales, there are a number of companies you can begin researching. Here's a list of some of the top players in order to help get you started.

TICKETMASTER

The gold standard against which all ticket agencies are judged, Ticketmaster was founded in Arizona in 1976 and is now headquartered in West Hollywood, California. Over the years, they have acquired many smaller ticket agencies, including Live Nation.

LIVE NATION

Considered the largest concert promoter, Live Nation merged with Ticketmaster in 2009 to form Live Nation Entertainment. Live Nation doesn't deal in sports ticket sales, but a job at Live Nation would be a great springboard for a job at Ticketmaster.

INTERVIEW WITH SARA THOMPSON, FORMER CUSTOMER SERVICE REPRESENTATIVE AT STUBHUB

Walk me through a typical day at work.

A day in the life of a StubHub employee was full of repetition, but with some [curveballs] thrown in. There was always something going on, whether it be website malfunctions, game cancellations or delays, invalid tickets, you name it. For the most part, I was answering questions from ticket buyers about when they would receive their tickets, what to do if something were to happen to the event, and [so on]. I would also help new sellers list their tickets.

We sold tickets to almost every [type of] event under the sun—even tickets to see the Dalai Lama. However, the vast majority of sales were for sporting events. Probably well over 50 percent. When I worked there, StubHub was integrated with MLB, so buying and selling tickets was extremely easy and seamless.

How do you think your experience at Stub-Hub helped prepare you for other jobs?

It helped me learn how to interact with people when we're not face to face, and how to keep my cool when someone was upset. It also helped me learn how to use certain programs better, like the Microsoft Office Suite.

What was the most challenging part of your job?

The challenges of my job changed day to day. At first, it was learning the procedures and programs. There was a lot to learn. After that, it was learning more about the sports teams.

What advice would you give someone who wants to work for StubHub or a similar agency?

Stay passionate and work on your interpersonal skills. Make an impression by putting out good work even when the job seems daunting or mundane. If you want to work within ticket sales or the secondary ticket market, it's all about keeping your excitement high.

ACE TICKET

Based in Boston, Massachusetts, Ace Ticket is considered one of the top ticket providers in the country. For buyers, Ace Ticket offers perks like free pickup and a customer loyalty rewards program. For full-time employees, Ace Ticket promises medical and dental insurance, 401(k), and "upward mobility" within your first year—not too shabby.

StubHub—founded in 2000 and owned by eBay—is not only one of the most popular ticket resellers . . . they're also a major sports sponsor.

STUBHUB

Owned by eBay, Stub-Hub is a truly innovative marketplace—the largest ticket marketplace, as well as the first company to debut many customer perks, like interactive seat mapping and technology that determines what tickets are really the best value. StubHub also partners with MLB, NHL, and others. They also give back to the community through their Rising Stars nonprofit recognition program—what's not to like?

Chapter 7
SPORTS ADVERTISING

Think of the last time you heard an ad on the radio advertising your favorite team or sporting event. Not only did someone have to write, record, edit, and produce that ad, but they also had to sell that airtime. If you're good with sales, a people person, and passionate about sports, a job as an advertising account executive might be for you.

SPORTS ADVERTISING 101

Let's say you like people but hate the bright overhead lights and busywork inherent with working at a sporting goods store. Maybe you're more of a creative type than you are a workhorse—content to spend a few hours scribbling in a notebook, but not really happy having to haul around boxes, stock shelves, or work a

First opened in 1912, Fenway Park is a bustling ballpark and home of the Boston Red Sox.

cash register. Maybe you thrive under the pressure of a deadline. If that's the case, a job in advertising might be more your speed.

Imagine coming into work and sitting down at your desk to make some phone calls. You might follow up with someone you met a few days ago to see if he or she had a chance to consider your offer, or you might make some cold calls—an unsolicited

PUTTING TOGETHER A WRITING PORTFOLIO

Before you even sit down to apply for your first advertising job, you'll need something above and beyond the standard résumé and cover letter. You'll need a writing portfolio.

Even if your interviewers don't ask for one, bringing a writing portfolio to a job interview will really give you a leg up on the competition. When creating your portfolio, don't splurge on fancy leather covers or anything like that—you're going to leave your portfolio with the interviewer. Don't expect to see it again.

A writing portfolio is a lot like a skills reel or highlight reel, only a portfolio showcases your writing chops instead of your physical abilities. Try to vary the types of writing you include. When in doubt, a profile (of a company or a person), a press release, some persuasive writing, a short script, and some example social media posts would be a good place to start. Keep in mind, you don't have to sit down and write those all right now, either; take a look at some of your past homework assignments for inspiration. Maybe you already have some pieces you can tweak and use. Once you've selected your pieces, write a brief explanation for each one, including what the desired audience and effect was for each piece.

Finally, write up a table of contents, make sure your pages are numbered correctly, print out all your pieces—including your résumé and cover letter—and bind them all together. You'll have a cool little booklet that showcases your writing strengths and talents—that's something to be proud of. Be sure to go back and update it periodically when you write new things that you're really proud of or that showcase a different area of your skills.

call, usually to a phone number that was given to you by another client. You might deal with smaller local teams to start, honing your skills and getting an idea of what works and what doesn't in the world of television, radio, and print, before branching out to deal with larger, better-established events and teams. You might write and rewrite a script, running it by your mentor with each revision, or you might listen to clips of voice talent, trying to select the exact right person to make your client's team sound great.

You may not always need a portfolio while interviewing for jobs, but you'll seem much more professional if you arrive at an interview well prepared.

INTERVIEW WITH TONY LAPPONESE, ACCOUNT EXECUTIVE AT CUMULUS BROADCASTING, LLC.

Tell us a little bit about your job.

I sell advertising [ad space] to businesses. [ESPN is] the only station in western Massachusetts to [broadcast] the Celtics, so if [I] find Celtics or basketball fans, [it's easy to sell ad space to them] because they are passionate about their teams. Passion sales are easy. I [also] cold-call. I do get some leads from people who call in [to the radio station]. I listen to other stations to see who is advertising with them. I get leads from Business West. I go through the value pack mailings, pay attention to billboards. I'll walk into businesses as well. I am a people person, so I find I am better [face-to-face] than I am on the phone. My job is to find someone's pain [point] — [how they might] need help with their business — and then offer a solution.

What exactly does it mean to sell ad space or airtime?

Once I secure a meeting and find their pain [point], the next step is to write a spec spot and bring it with a proposal. A spec spot is a recording of what a commercial would sound like for them. I need to get them involved, get them excited. Then I say, "Here is what you would get for x amount of dollars."

What advice would you have for someone who wants to work in sports?
Take broadcasting [courses] in school and intern at any local TV or radio station you can. I can't tell you how many interns I had for my show over the years that have gotten sports broadcasting jobs. Coming out of school, the only experience you can possibly get is from an internship, and they are incredibly helpful.

NETWORK, NETWORK, NETWORK

Networking is very important when it comes to lots of jobs, and this holds true for advertising, too. Being a successful networker is all about connecting, being friendly, and solving other people's problems ... while sometimes also helping yourself. Always stay on good terms with people, keep any business cards you may receive (and jot down key details on the back of them to help you remember that person), and introduce people to others, if appropriate. If you know Jim is an accountant who wants to learn to play tennis, and later on you meet Jane, who is a tennis instruc-

Although it may feel awkward at first, networking will always come in handy . . . no matter what type of career you decide to pursue.

tor who's struggling to organize her taxes ... introduce them to each other. People will be grateful for your help and thrilled that you remembered them and their needs— and they'll almost always remember you and return the favor when they can.

Chapter 8
GYM FRONT DESK

If your love of sports extends to a passion for physical fitness, working the front desk at a gym might be a great fit for you. Part greeter, part cashier, and part cleanup crew, a job at a gym pretty much guarantees you'll never get bored.

RUNNING THE FRONT DESK

First and foremost, working the front desk at a gym means that you are the first point of contact for all gym patrons. This means a cheery, friendly disposition goes a long way. Though you may sometimes share duties with other team members (generally depending on how busy your shift is and the size of the gym), most of the time, you'll be responsible for greeting patrons, explaining various membership packages and signing new customers up for them, and wiping down machines. You might be expected to help schedule personal trainer appointments for patrons, too, and make some occasional phone calls.

Tech skills are always in demand. Here, a front desk clerk uses a laptop to help sign customers up for gym memberships.

Some larger, more expensive gyms offer lots of amenities, including swimming pools, tanning beds, saunas, aromatherapy rooms, and even cafés. At these larger gyms, you may find yourself running the smoothie counter, programming the tanning beds, or doling out towels for the pool. Some gyms offer daycare, and some even organize birthday parties, where you might be expected to run out and get a cake, hang decorations, or referee a volleyball game. All in all, when working at a gym, it helps to be friendly and flexible.

INTERVIEW WITH KATIE MCDONNELL, FORMER FRONT DESK ASSOCIATE AT HEALTHTRAX

What made you first decide to apply for a job at a gym?

I really liked their hours. I was a junior in high school, and it was nice that I could work after school—and the free membership was a bonus. I liked meeting new people and being able to chat with [them]. It was nice to be part of a community like that.

Was any special training required for this job?

We didn't need any specific special training besides on-the-job training, [but] the personal trainers were all certified, so they [did have] special training.

You're a big fan of the New England Patriots. Did that ever come into play at work?

Not really, [but] a lot of the local high school sport teams came in, so it definitely made me pay attention to their schedule and chat with them about their season. For example, since we had a pool, [members] of the girls swim team would come in to work out. I made sure to listen to the sports announcements to see if they won so I could congratulate them when I saw them.

What was the most rewarding part of your job?

The best part was forming relationships with people. I had a great time talking with the trainers and got *very close to the membership office. The clients got to know us and would make a point to ask about school, getting into college, prom, etc.*

How did your job as a front desk associate help prepare you for the future?
It [taught me] great customer service skills, [and] it was great to have free access to a health club membership. I loved to see people accomplishing their fitness goals, too—it was very motivating. A lot of people can be scared to join a gym, so it [also] helped take away that anxiety.

PERSONAL TRAINING

After some time spent working at the front desk and chatting with your coworkers, you might find yourself enjoying the overall gym environment but wanting a role that's more involved when it comes to health and fitness. If your passion lies more in fitness than in customer service, and you want to work more closely with clients to help them meet their goals, maybe you'd be interested in a job as a personal trainer.

EDUCATION

To work as a personal trainer, you need to become certified. But before you can do that, there are a few prerequisites. You'll

One way personal trainers help is by "spotting" their clients. Their assistance helps guide clients to use the proper form, thereby preventing potentially serious injury.

need to be eighteen years old, have a high school diploma or a GED, and hold an active CPR certification.

Once those are out of the way, you'll need to choose a program to enroll in. There are a number of different programs that offer personal trainer certifications, including the American Council on Exercise, the American College of Sports Medicine, and the National Academy of Sports Medicine. Check with the gym you want to work for to see if they recommend a certification—some gyms have preferences. Also, if you already work for a gym and your managers know you're looking to get certified, they might have scholarships available, so be sure they're aware of your interest.

After your classes are paid for, all you have left to do is study and pass your exams … then you'll be certified and ready to work.

BE YOUR OWN BOSS

With a personal trainer certification, you don't necessarily have to work in a gym, either—if you have big dreams and are a self-starter, you can market yourself and work as a private personal trainer. Imagine working out of your home or maybe having your own office, meeting up with clients, and being your own boss … does that sound good to you? If that's something you want to plan for, just keep two things in mind. First, you'll need to carry some kind of liability insurance if you're working on your own—if you were employed by a gym as a personal trainer, you were covered under the gym's insurance, but as a self-employed trainer, you'll need to purchase your own policy. Don't skimp on this, either… It's absolutely crucial to make sure you're covered in the unlikely event that one of your clients gets injured while you're training with him or her.

Being self-employed, you'll need to do your taxes a little differently, too. While others file their taxes once a year, self-employed workers are responsible

As a freelancer, you'll be responsible for keeping close track of your finances—be sure you set aside some money for tax time.

for filing quarterly taxes—that means they need to file once every quarter, four times a year. If taxes and numbers boggle your mind, you may want to enlist the help of an accountant or tax specialist. In the meantime, make sure you keep detailed notes on how much money you're bringing in so that you are able to calculate exactly how much you owe to Uncle Sam.

COLLEGE AND UNIVERSITY PROGRAMS IN SPORTS RETAIL

Auburn University
Auburn, Alabama 36849
(334) 844-4000
Website: https://www
.auburn.edu
Programs of study: Exercise
science, nutrition, physical education

Florida State University
600 W. College Avenue
Tallahassee, FL 32306
(850) 644-2525
Website: http://www.fsu.edu
Programs of study: Dietetics, athletic training,
human sciences, retail
merchandising, exercise
physiology

Louisiana State University
Enrollment Management
1146 Pleasant Hall
Baton Rouge, LA 70803
(225) 578-1175
Website: http://www.lsu.edu
/index.php
Programs of study: Athletic
training, kinesiology,
dietetics, sports adminis-
tration

Ohio State University
281 W. Lane Avenue
Columbus, OH 43210
(614) 292-3980
Website: https://www.osu
.edu
Programs of study:
Athletic training; exer-
cise science education;
health promotion,
nutrition, and exercise
science; physical educa-
tion

University of Alabama
Undergraduate Admissions
The University of Alabama
203 Student Services Center
Box 870132
Tuscaloosa, AL 35487
(205) 348-5666
Website: https://www.ua.edu
Programs of study: Physi-
cal education, exercise
and sport science, athletic
training, food and nutri-
tion

University of Florida
University of Florida Office of Admissions
201 Criser Hall, PO Box 114000, University of Florida
Gainesville, FL 32611-4000
(352) 392-1365
Website: http://www.ufl.edu
Programs of study: Applied physiology and kinesiology, athletic training, dance, dietetics, food science, health education and behavior, health science, marketing, nutritional science, sport management

University of Maryland
College Park, MD 20742
(301) 405-1000
Website: https://umd.edu
Programs of study: Kinesiology, nutrition and food science

University of Michigan
Ann Arbor
Office of Undergraduate Admissions
515 East Jefferson Street, 1220 Student Activities Building
Ann Arbor, MI 48109
(734) 764-7433
Website: https://www.umich.edu
Programs of study: Athletic training, dance, health and fitness, movement science, sport management

University of Oklahoma
660 Parrington Oval
Norman, OK 73019
(405) 325-0311
Website: https://www.ou.edu
Programs of study: Health and exercise science

University of Texas at Austin
Office of Admissions
PO Box 8058
Austin, TX 78713
(512) 475-7399
Website: http://www.utexas.edu
Programs of study: Athletic training, kinesiology and health education, sport management, nutrition

A CAREER IN SPORTS RETAIL AT A GLANCE

SPORTS MEMORABILIA RETAIL

ACADEMICS

High school diploma or higher

EXPERIENCE

Internship or volunteer experience may be helpful
Customer service skills desirable

CAREER PATHS

A customer service associate or salesperson may be able to work up to supervisor, assistant manager, or manager … or may choose to open his or her own shop one day.

RESPONSIBILITIES

Keeping up with current events in the sports world
Running a cash register
Stocking shelves

Dealing with customers

Ordering and listing items online

SPORTING GOODS RETAIL

ACADEMICS

High school diploma or higher

EXPERIENCE

Internship or volunteer experience may be helpful

Customer service skills desirable

CAREER PATHS

A customer service associate or salesperson may be able to work up to supervisor, assistant manager, or manager... or may choose to open his or her own shop one day.

RESPONSIBILITIES

Gaining a working knowledge of all products and departments

Running a cash register

Stocking shelves, counting inventory, and ordering new stock

Dealing with customers

SEASON PASSES/TICKET SALES

ACADEMICS

High school diploma or higher

EXPERIENCE

Internship or volunteer experience may be helpful
Customer service skills desirable, including answering telephones
Computer skills required

CAREER PATHS

Large ticket agencies have various departments you could transfer into, and there are always opportunities for promotion.

RESPONSIBILITIES

Keeping up with current events in the sports world
Answering telephones
Processing orders and listing tickets

SPORTS ADVERTISING

ACADEMICS

High school diploma or higher

EXPERIENCE

Internship or volunteer experience may be helpful

Strong writing and public speaking skills desirable

Good interpersonal skills a plus

CAREER PATHS

A job in sports advertising allows for lateral mobility as well as upward. You could transition into broadcasting, editing, or even managing other account executives.

RESPONSIBILITIES

Keeping up with current events in the sports world

Cold-calling

Writing spec scripts

Maintaining relationships with customers

GYM FRONT DESK

ACADEMICS

High school diploma or higher

EXPERIENCE

Internship or volunteer experience may be helpful but not required

Customer service skills desirable

CAREER PATHS

A customer service associate or salesperson may be able to work his or her way up to supervisor, assistant manager, or manager… or may choose to open his or her own shop one day.

RESPONSIBILITIES

Greeting guests

Light paperwork

Answering telephones

Occasional cleaning duties

Some gyms may have you set up and break down for events, like birthday parties

WHAT SPORTS RETAIL EMPLOYEES DO

Sports retail sales workers include both those who sell retail merchandise, such as clothing, shoes, sporting goods and equipment, and tickets to sporting events. These retail sales workers help customers find the products they want and process customers' payments.

WORK ENVIRONMENT

Most sports retail sales workers work in clean, well-lit stores. Many sales workers work evenings and weekends.

HOW TO BECOME A SPORTS RETAIL EMPLOYEE

Typically, there are no formal education requirements for sports retail sales workers. Most receive on-the-job training, which usually lasts a few days to a few months.

PAY AND JOB OUTLOOK

The salaries and projections for jobs within the sports retail industry change from month to month and can also vary greatly depending on your education and what area you live in. (Larger cities with a professional sports team will have a better customer base for memorabilia. Towns with a booming tourism industry for camping or outdoor sports will have a better customer base for sporting goods.) For the most complete and up-to-date list of salary information, always refer to the Bureau of Labor Statistics website.

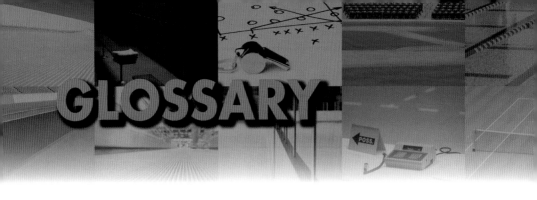

GLOSSARY

ad space Physical blank space in printed media—such as newspapers or magazines—where ads can be placed.

airtime Portions of time on the radio during which ads can be aired.

brick and mortar Referring to a store or company that has a physical location versus an online-only shop.

cold-calling Solicitation of business from potential customers who have had no prior contact with the salesperson conducting the call.

commission An amount of money paid to the salesperson after he or she successfully closes a sale.

future proof The process of anticipating future needs and planning ahead to minimize the effects of future events.

in-house Someone who works within an organization, rather than an external or freelance worker.

intramural Recreational sports organized within an educational institution or geographic area.

leads Prospective customers who are suggested by others.

marketing The action or business of promoting and selling products or services, including market research and advertising.

NAIA National Association of Intercollegiate Athletics, an athletic association that organizes college and university-level athletic programs in the United States and beyond.

NCAA The National Collegiate Athletic Association, a non-profit association that organizes the athletic programs of many colleges and universities in the United States and Canada.

pain point A problem that a client or customer is having.

retail The sale of goods to the public in relatively small quantities for use or consumption rather than for resale.

sales The act of selling.

Southeastern Conference An American college athletic conference consisting of colleges primarily in the southern United States.

spec spot A thirty-second unpaid commercial sample.

traffic Material that is aired on the radio.

walk-on When an athlete becomes part of a team without being recruited or awarded an academic scholarship.

FOR MORE INFORMATION

Athletics Canada

2445, Saint Laurent Boulevard

Ottawa, ON K1G 6C3

Canada

(613) 260-5580

Website: http://athletics.ca

Facebook: @AthleticsCanada

Twitter: @AthleticsCanada

Instagram: @AthleticsCanada

Athletics Canada is the national sport governing body for track and field. Athletics Canada supports high-performance athletics excellence at the world level and provides leadership in developmental athletics.

Institut national du sport du Québec

4141, Avenue Pierre-De-Coubertin

Montréal, QC H1V 3N7

Canada

Website: https://www.insquebec.org

Facebook: @INSQuebec

Twitter: @INSQuebec

The Institut national du sport du Québec (INS Québec) provides athletes and coaches with support in order to help "lead them to excellence."

National Association of Intercollegiate Athletics (NAIA)

1200 Grand Boulevard

Kansas City, MO 64106

Website: http://naia.org

Twitter: @NAIA_news

The National Association of Intercollegiate Athletics is the governing body of small athletics programs that are dedicated to character-driven intercollegiate athletics.

National Association of Sports Commissions

9916 Carver Road, Suite 100

Cincinnati, OH 45242

Website: https://www.sportscommissions.org

Facebook: @SportsCommissions

Twitter: @NASC_News

Instagram: @SportsCommissions

Aiming to help sport tourism "transform society for the better," the National Association of Sports Commissions helps by providing their members with valuable education and networking opportunities.

National Collegiate Athletic Association (NCAA)

1802 Alonzo Watford Sr. Drive

Indianapolis, IN 46202

Website: http://www.ncaa.com and http://www.ncaa.org

Facebook: @ncaastudents

Twitter: @NCAA

The National Collegiate Athletic Association is an organization dedicated to the well-being and lifelong success of college athletes.

Team USA

United States Olympic Committee

One Olympic Plaza

Colorado Springs, CO 80909

Website: http://www.teamusa.org/About-the-USOC

Facebook: @TeamUSA

Twitter: @TeamUSA

Instagram: @TeamUSA

The United States Olympic Committee's goal is to support US Olympic and Paralympic athletes. They provide the training and funding for US Olympic teams.

WEBSITES

Because of the changing nature of Internet links, Rosen Publishing has developed an online list of websites related to the subject of this book. This site is updated regularly. Please use this link to access the list:

http://www.rosenlinks.com/GCSI/Retail

FOR FURTHER READING

ACE personal trainer certification exam prep team. *ACE Personal Trainer Study Guide: Study Companion & Practice Test Questions for the American Council on Exercise Personal Trainer Certification Exam.* N.p.: CreateSpace Independent Publishing Platform, 2015.

Alexander, Kwame. *Crossover.* Boston, MA: Houghton Mifflin Harcourt, 2017.

Alexander, Kwame, and Thai Neave. *The Playbook: 52 Rules to Aim, Shoot, and Score in This Game Called Life.* Boston, MA: Houghton Mifflin Harcourt, 2017.

Benedict, Jeff. *The System: The Glory and Scandal of Big-Time College Football.* New York, NY: Random House, 2014.

Biles, Simone. *Courage to Soar: A Body in Motion, a Life in Balance.* New York, NY: HarperCollins Christian Publishers, 2016.

Bryant, Cedric X., and Daniel J. Green. *ACE's Essentials of Exercise Science for Fitness Professionals.* San Diego, CA: American Council on Exercise, 2012.

Christen, Carol, and Richard Nelson Bolles. *What Color Is Your Parachute? For Teens: Discover Yourself, Design Your Future, and Plan for Your Dream Job.* Berkeley, CA: Ten Speed Press, 2015.

Currie, Stephen. *Teen Guide to Jobs and Taxes.* San Diego, CA: ReferencePoint Press, Inc., 2017.

Doepke, Darrell. *The Part-Timer Primer: A Teen's Guide*

to Surviving the Hiring Process and Landing Your First Job. Sammamish, WA: Timbrewolfe Publishing, 2012.

Douglas, Gabrielle, and Michelle Burford. *Grace, Gold and Glory: My Leap of Faith*. Grand Rapids, MI: Zondervan, 2013.

Goodman, Jonathan. *Ignite the Fire: The Secrets to Building a Successful Personal Training Career*. N.p.: CreateSpace, 2015.

Gordon, Jon. *You Win in the Locker Room First: 7 C's to Build a Winning Team in Sports, Business and Life*. Hoboken, NJ: Wiley, 2015.

Grant, Mick, and John Molvar. *The Youth and Teen Running Encyclopedia: A Complete Guide for Middle and Long Distance Runners Ages 6 to 18*. N.p.: Createspace, 2014.

Ivy, John, and Robert Portman. *The Performance Zone: Your Nutrition Action Plan for Greater Endurance & Sports Performance*. Columbus, OH: Basic Health Publications, 2013.

Joyce, Dru, Chris Morrow, and LeBron James. *Beyond Championships: A Playbook for Winning at Life*. Grand Rapids, MI: Zondervan, 2015.

Kiyosak, Robert T., and Sharon L. Lechter. *Rich Dad Poor Dad for Teens*. Philadelphia, PA: Running Press, 2009.

Licht, Aliza. *Leave Your Mark: Land Your Dream Job. Kill It in Your Career. Rock Social Media*. New York, NY: Grand Central Publishing, 2015.

Lyons, Douglas B. *100 Years of Who's Who in Baseball*. Guilford, CT: Lyons Press, 2015.

Mooney, Carla. *Cool Careers Without College for People*

Who Love Sports. New York, NY: Rosen Publishing, 2017.

Rau, Dana Meachen. *Sports Nutrition for Teen Athletes: Eat Right to Take Your Game to the Next Level.* North Mankato, MN: Capstone Press, 2012.

Standard Catalog of Vintage Baseball Cards. Iola, WI: Krause Publications, 2016

Wong, Stephen, and Dave Grob. *Game Worn: Baseball Treasures from the Game's Greatest Heroes and Moments.* Washington, DC: Smithsonian, 2016.

BIBLIOGRAPHY

Allenspach, Kevin. "What's it like to run a sports memorabilia business?" St. Cloud Times. January 19, 2015. http://www.sctimes.com/story/life/2015/01/19/like-run-sports-memorabilia-business/22009351.

American Council on Exercise. *ACE Personal Trainer Study Guide: Study Companion & Practice Test Questions for the American Council on Exercise Personal Trainer Certification Exam.* United States: Test Prep Books, 2016.

American Council on Exercise. "Personal Trainer Certification." ACE Fitness. Retrieved April 13, 2017. https://www.acefitness.org/fitness-certifications/personal-trainer-certification/default.aspx.

Burns, Mark J. "How To Land Your Dream Job In Sports." Forbes. July 11, 2016. https://www.forbes.com/sites/markjburns/2016/07/10/how-to-land-your-dream-job-in-sports/#4ff752f579c7.

Castle, Jill. *Eat like a Champion: Performance Nutrition for Your Young Athlete.* New York, NY: American Management Association, 2015.

Christen, Carol. *What Color is Your Parachute? For Teens: Discover Yourself, Design Your Future, and Plan for Your Dream Job.* Berkeley, CA: Ten Speed Press, 2015.

Doepke, Darrell. *The Part-timer Primer: A Teen's Guide to Surviving the Hiring Process and Landing Your First Job.* Sammamish, WA: Timbrewolfe Publishing, 2012.

Gaines, Melinda. "How to Start a Sports Memorabilia Business." Chron.com. October 14, 2010. http://smallbusiness.chron.com/start-sports-memorabilia-business-2148.html.

Hagerman, Adam. "Confessions of a Retail Salesman: Beware of These 4 Sales Tactics." Man vs. Debt. Retrieved April 13, 2017. http://manvsdebt.com/confessions-of-a-retail-salesman-beware-of-these-4-sales-tactics/.

Kennedy, Kostya. "Even After 25 Years, Pete Rose's Ban From Baseball Is Money in the Bank." FiveThirtyEight. July 31, 2014. https://fivethirtyeight.com/features/even-after-25-years-pete-roses-ban-from-baseball-is-money-in-the-bank/.

Kennedy, Kostya. *Pete Rose: an American Dilemma*. New York, NY: *Sports Illustrated*, an imprint of Time Home Entertainment, Inc., 2014.

Licht, Aliza. *Leave Your Mark: Land Your Dream Job. Kill it in Your Career. Rock Social Media*. New York, NY: Grand Central Publishing, 2015.

MediaMonitors, and Specbyte. "Radio is Best Sold When Played, Not Pitched." Insideradio.com. May 4, 2015. http://www.insideradio.com/features/must_read_mondays/radio-is-best-sold-when-played-not-pitched/article_5fcd7d76-f026-11e4-b02b-3354eb7c695c.html.

Michaels, Al, and L. Jon Wertheim. *You Can't Make This Up: Miracles, Memories, and the Perfect Marriage of Sports and Television*. New York, NY: William Morrow, 2015.

Niche. "2017 Best College Athletics." Niche.com. Retrieved April 13, 2017. https://www.niche.com/colleges/rankings/best-college-athletics.

Rodenberg, Ryan. "Pete Rose's Reckless Gamble." Atlantic Media Company. August 22, 2014. https://www

.theatlantic.com/entertainment/archive/2014/08
/why-pete-rose-still-cant-be-absolved/378866.

SportsMemorabilia.com. "A Comprehensive Guide to
Collecting Sports Memorabilia." SportsMemorabilia.com.
Retrieved April 13, 2017. http://www.sportsmemorabilia
.com/resources/sports-memorabilia-101.html.

Stringfield, Bradley. "Tips to Creating a Highlight Video
Package That Will Catch a College Recruiter's Eye." Youth
Football. Retrieved April 14, 2017. https://web
.usafootball.com/blogs/u.s.-national-team/post/10959
/tips-to-creating-a-highlight-video-package-that-will
-catch-a-college-recruiter%27s-eye.

Steck, Emily. "How To Create a Killer Writing Portfolio for
Freelancers." Quietly Blog. November 19, 2015. https://
blog.quiet.ly/community
/how-to-create-a-writing-portfolio-for-freelancers.

Steinberg, Leigh. "5 Keys To Getting A Job In Sports." Forbes.
May 24, 2016. https://www.forbes.com/sites
/leighsteinberg/2016/05/12/5-keys-to-getting-a-job-in
-sports/#6365cf69310c.

Steiner, Brandon. *You Gotta Have Balls: How a Kid from
Brooklyn Started from Scratch, Bought Yankee Stadium, and
Created a Sports Empire.* Hoboken, NJ: Wiley, 2012.

Tkaczyk, Christopher. "Looking for Work? Here are 20 Great
Employers in the Retail Industry." Fortune.com. November
20, 2014. http://fortune
.com/2014/11/19/20-great-workplaces-in-retail.

West Virginia University. "Breaking into College Sports." Well
.wvu.edu. April 13, 2017. http://well.wvu.edu/articles
/breaking_into_college_sports.

INDEX

A

Ace Ticket, 80, 83, 87
Alabama, University of, 52
Auburn University, 52

B

Baylor University , 52

C

cable access stations, activities
    there to help aspiring sports
    retailers, 26, 28, 30
California, Los Angeles,
    University of, 37, 39
CareerBuilder, 10, 84
clothing, choosing professional
    and appropriate, 34, 84
club sports teams, 50
coaching, 24, 26, 31–32
cold calls, 91
college
    courses to take, 34
    picking a school, 36–37, 39,
        41–42
    sports opportunities in, 48, 50
    top twenty colleges for ath-
        letes, 51–52

Connecticut

Connecticut, University of,
    37, 52
cover letter, 11, 92
Cumulus Broadcasting, 94–95

D

Dick's Sporting Goods, 7, 70–71
Duke University, 52

E

e-commerce retail, profile of a
    company, 74–75
employee benefits, 74–75
equipment manager, 24

F

Facebook, 15, 16
Florida, University of, 36–37, 52
Florida State University, 52

G

grooming, 33
gym front desk associate
    day-to-day duties of, 97–98
    interview with an associate,
        99–100

H

Hagerman, Adam, 15
Healthtrax, 99–100
high school, courses to take, 34–35

I

Indeed.com, 10, 84
internships, 26, 30, 32, 33, 36
intramural sports, 50, 53

J

job interviews, tips for getting, 10–11
job listings, websites for, 10, 84

K

Kentucky, University of, 52

L

Lapponese, Tony, 94–95
Live Nation, 85
Louisville, University of, 52

M

major, how to choose one, 42, 44–46
marketing
   as a college major, 45–46
   how it differs from sales, 12, 14–15
Maryland, College Park, University of, 52

McDonnell, Katie, 99–100
Miami, University of, 52
Michaels, Al, 23–24
Michigan, University of, 37, 52
Michigan State University, 37, 52

N

National Basketball Association (NBA), 81
National Collegiate Athletic Association (NCAA), 36, 39, 40, 48, 50
neurology, as a college major, 44
North Carolina at Chapel Hill, University of, 52
nutrition, as a college major, 42, 44

O

Ohio State University, 52
Oklahoma, University of, 52

P

Parisi, Michael, 70–71
parks and recreation departments, activities there to help aspiring sports retailers, 26
personal trainer, education and skills required to be one, 99, 100–103
physiology, as a college major, 45
Pro Athlete, 74–75
psychology, as a college major, 44

R

rate/price, determining what to charge, 16
résumé, 10, 32, 41, 92
retail, how it differs from sales and marketing, 12, 14–15
retail management, as a college major, 45
Rose, Pete, 57

S

sales, how they differ from retail and marketing, 12, 14–15
scholarships, 21, 34, 40–41
school, activities there to help aspiring sports retailers, 24
school newspaper, 23 , 24, 48, 53, 54
self-employment, 102–103
SnagAJob.com, 10
social media specialists, what they do, 16–17
softball coach, interview with, 31–32
Southern California, University of, 52
spectating, 55
sporting goods sales
    day-to-day duties, 12, 14, 67, 69, 73, 75, 77–79
    interview with a retail associate, 70–71

sports advertising
    importance of networking in, 95–96
    interview with an account executive, 94–95
    job responsibilities in, 11, 90–91, 93
sports memorabilia sales
    day-to-day duties, 56–58, 60
    detecting fraud, 60, 62
    interview with a shop owner, 61–62
    types of memorabilia sold, 63, 65–66
sports retail
    overview of industry, 7, 9, 11–12
    technology used in, 17, 19–20
statistics classes, 34
Steiner, Brandon, 61–62, 66
StubHub, 80, 86–87, 89
student media, 53–55
Sullivan, Christie, 31–32

T

Tennessee, University of, 52
Texas A&M University, 52
Texas at Austin, University of, 52
Thompson, Sara, 86
Ticketmaster, 85

ticket sales companies
    getting a job, 83–84
    group ticket sales, 81–82, 85
    interview with a customer service rep, 86–87
    profiles of companies, 85, 87, 89
    resale agencies, 80
    strategic sales, 82
Twitter, 15

U

user experience design, 20

W

web development, 19–20
work-study opportunities, 46, 48
writing portfolio, assembling one, 92
writing skills, 34–35, 92

Y

You Can't Make This Up: Miracles, Memories, and the Perfect Marriage of Sports and Television, 24
YouTube, 16, 17

ABOUT THE AUTHOR

Alison Downs is a writer and editor living in the Boston area. Downs's fiction, poetry, and essays have appeared widely online and in print, including in *Big Pulp* magazine, *Meat for Tea: The Valley Review*, and HelloGiggles.com. Downs holds a BFA in creative writing and an MA in English.

PHOTO CREDITS

Cover, p. 1 Disability Images/Blend Images/Getty Images; cover, p. 1 (background) August 0802/Shutterstock.com; p. 4 Damian Strohmeyer /Sports Illustrated/Getty Images; pp. 8–9 Bloomberg/Getty Images; pp. 12–13 Kali9/E+/Getty Images; pp. 18–19 Robert Barnes/Moment Mobile/Getty Images; pp. 22–23 © iStockphoto.com/Asiseeit; pp. 25, 98 Jupiterimages/Stockbyte/Thinkstock; pp. 26–27 Jon Osumi /Shutterstock.com; pp. 28–29 Antb/Shutterstock.com; pp. 38–39 Icon Sports Wire/Getty Images; pp. 42–43 © iStockphoto.com/Skynesher; pp. 46–47 Trish233/iStock/Thinkstock; pp. 48–49 Andrea Baldo/ LightRocket/Getty Images; p. 53 Oleh Dubyna/Shutterstock.com; p. 54 Susan Montgomery/Shutterstock.com; p. 56 Boston Globe/Getty Images; pp. 58–59 John Greim/LightRocket/Getty Images; p. 63 Chicago Tribune/Getty Images; pp. 64–65 Rob Kim/Getty Images; pp. 68–69, 72–73 © iStockphoto.com/Extreme Photographer; pp. 76–77 © iStockphoto.com/4x6; p. 81 Mikhail Pochuyev/TASS/Getty Images; p. 82 © iStockphoto.com/SolStock; p. 83 Rawpixel/Shutterstock.com; pp. 88–89 DW labs Incorporated/Shutterstock.com; p. 91 Rick Friedman /Corbis Sport/Getty Images; p. 93 Wong Yu Liang/Shutterstock.com; p. 96 ASDF Media/Shutterstock.com; p. 101 LightField Studios /Shutterstock.com; p. 103 WayHome Studio/Shutterstock.com; interior design elements: © www.istockphoto.com/hudiemm (grid pattern); http://lostandtaken.com (striped border); pp. 7, 21, 36, 67, 80, 97, 104, 106, 111, 113, 115, 118 (montage) © www.iStockphoto.com, Shutterstock.com.

Design: Brian Garvey; Layout: Ellina Litmanovich;
Editor: Bethany Bryan; Photo Researcher: Sherri Jackson